4/23

WHAT IS
Coding?

BY MEG MARQUARDT

Published by The Child's World®
1980 Lookout Drive • Mankato, MN 56003-1705
800-599-READ • www.childsworld.com

Photographs ©: Shutterstock Images, cover (top boy), cover (food), cover (bottom boy), 1 (top boy), 1 (food), 1 (bottom boy), 6, 8, 9, 10, 19, 20, 24; Igor Aleks/Shutterstock Images, 5; Filipe Frazao/Shutterstock, 15; Getty Images Plus, 16

ISBN 9781503831957
LCCN 2018962802

Printed in the United States of America
PA02418

ABOUT THE AUTHOR

Meg Marquardt has been gaming since she was a little girl. Today, she loves to research and write about game design, E-Sport competitions, and more. She lives in Madison, Wisconsin, with her two scientist cats, Lagrange and Doppler.

TABLE OF CONTENTS

CHAPTER 1

What Is Computer Code?

Jared wants to make cupcakes for his mom's birthday. He pulls out the big recipe book. After flipping through a few pages, he finds the cupcake recipe.

He follows the recipe step-by-step. He mixes together flour and baking soda. He adds some cocoa powder. Then, he blends sugar, eggs, and butter. With a little milk and vanilla, the batter is ready to go.

The cupcakes go into the oven. The kitchen timer goes off after 30 minutes. Jared puts on oven mitts and grabs the tray out of the oven. Jared knows that he followed the recipe perfectly. He has 12 beautiful chocolate cupcakes!

In order to have 12 perfect cupcakes, Jared has to follow the recipe exactly.

5

A robot must read the code in its computer in order to do things.

Computer **code** is like a recipe. It tells a computer how to work. A computer reads a line of code just as a person reads a step in a recipe. It follows the instructions exactly. Code can direct a computer to do different things, such as control a robot. What that robot does is just like Jared's cupcakes. Its actions are the product at the end of the coding recipe.

CHAPTER 2

Thinking in Code

The first computers were basically very powerful **calculators**. People used computers to help them do math faster than they could by hand. Early computers worked with one type of code. That code is called **binary**.

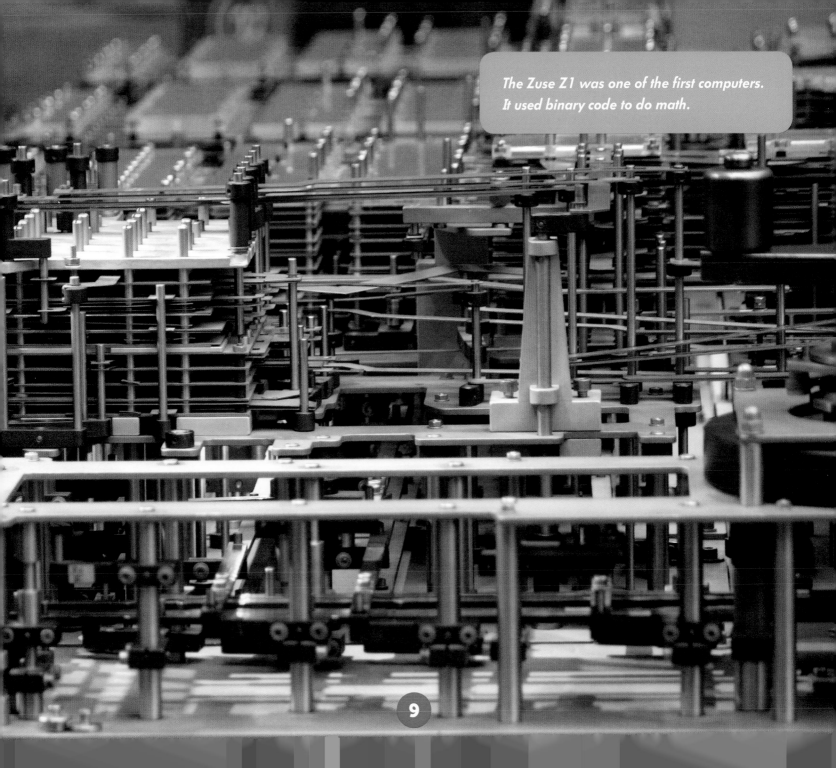

The Zuse Z1 was one of the first computers. It used binary code to do math.

Transistors are necessary parts of computers. They act like switches. Everything a computer does depends on which transistors are on or off.

Binary code uses only 1s and 0s. The 1s and 0s are like switches. Computers are made up of electronics called **transistors**. If a computer reads a 1, it knows to turn a transistor on. If the computer reads a 0, it knows to turn a transistor off. Turning different transistors on and off makes the computer do different things.

A computer is made up of billions of transistors. Imagine having to write long strings of code with billions of 1s and 0s for every step in a program. That would make coding very difficult!

As computers gained more transistors, **coders** realized they needed a simpler way to make a computer work. They invented coding languages, also called programming languages. Coding languages allow coders to talk to the computer without writing in binary code. Instead, the coder types commands with words and **symbols**. The coding language turns these commands into 1s and 0s for the computer to understand. Coding languages give coders more time to make up new and inventive code.

A coder wants the computer screen to display "Hello, World!" Coding this in binary takes many ones and zeros. Coding this in the language FORTRAN uses simple words.

Both types of code tell the computer to do the same thing. But it is much easier to write the program in a coding language than it is to write it in binary.

Binary

```
01001000 01100101 01101100
01101100 01101111 00101100
00100000 01010111 01101111
01110010 01101100 01100100
00100001
```

FORTRAN

```
program hello
print *, "Hello, World!"
end program hello
```

CHAPTER 3

Solving Problems Using Code

Code runs the world. Every electronic device uses code. Computers, phones, and even cars are powered by code. Coders can write code that does just about anything. They use different coding languages to solve different problems.

People use code to run websites. For example, a travel agency is setting up a new website. It only books hotels in the United States, Canada, and Mexico. A coder could use the coding language Ruby to tell the website to only search for hotels in those countries.

Smartphones run on code. They are small computers that can fit in your pocket.

Code controls every element of the video games people play.

One way people use code is to sort through **databases**. A database is a place that stores lots of information. For example, a school's database will have students' names and class schedules. A principal might want to know which students are taking music. Code in languages like SQL and PHP would quickly search the database and pull up a list of those students.

Code also helps people have fun. Video games are built with code. Game designers use coding languages like Java and C++ to build every aspect of a game. Code is used to add images and music. Code even controls how characters walk, talk, and battle.

Code can also be used to make the world a better place. Some coders make **apps** that help people in need. For example, in the country of Uganda, some farmers' crops were getting sick. Coders at Makerere University in Uganda made an app that could take pictures of these crops. The app would then tell the farmers if the crops were healthy or sick. Coders used code to create this app, which helped farmers across the country. Other apps help people all over the world. Coding is an important part of society.

Farmers can use apps to help them grow their crops.

Q: What is binary?

A: Binary is the basic computer coding language.

Q: What is binary made up of?

    a. 1s and 0s

    b. 2s and 3s

    c. words

    d. symbols

A: a. 1s and 0s

Q: What coding language is good for creating video games?

    a. Java

    b. SQL

    c. C++

    d. both a and c

A: d. both a and c

Q: Why do we need different coding languages?

A: Different coding languages solve different problems.

apps (APS) Apps are programs for phones, tablets, and computers. Coders create apps that help people.

binary (BYE-nayr-ee) Binary is the most basic computer coding language. Binary is the coding language made up of 1s and 0s.

calculators (KAL-kyoo-lay-turz) Calculators are tools that solve math problems. Early computers were like calculators.

code (KOHD) Code is a list of instructions that computers follow to do things. The computer follows code that makes it play music.

coders (KOHD-urz) Coders are people who write code. Coders create video games.

databases (DAY-tuh-bay-sez) Databases are places where information is stored. Principals can use databases to search for students' in classes.

symbols (SIM-bulz) Symbols are characters on the keyboard that are not numbers or letters. Coders use symbols such as * when they write code.

transistors (tran-ZISS-turz) Transistors control the flow of electricity in a computer. The number 1 in binary turns transistors on.

TO LEARN MORE

IN THE LIBRARY

Kelly, James Floyd. *The Story of Coding*.
New York, NY: DK Publishing, 2017.

Wainewright, Max. *I'm an App Developer*. New
York, NY: Crabtree Publishing, 2017.

Woodcock, Jon. *DK Workbooks: Computer Coding*.
New York, NY: DK Publishing, 2014.

ON THE WEB

Visit our website for links about coding:
childsworld.com/links

INDEX